DUSTY SPRINGFIELD

Complete look into the life of soul singer
Mary Isobel
Catherine

Amelia Pedro

TABLE OF CONTENT

INTRODUCTION

When I was a youngster, I first became aware of Dusty's mysterious influence when listening to heartfelt ballads like "I Close My Eyes and H Count to Ten" and "You Don't Have to Say You Love Me," and it felt like there was this lovely, dejected lady singing from a distance across a room. A remarkable appearance, including silver-blonde hair in a bouffant style, delicate features, and thickly mascaraed eyes, added to the impression of longing.

Dusty was a fascinating puzzle. With a number of UK hit singles, she enjoyed a decade of sweet stardom in the 1960s. She then traveled to America and vanished. What transpired?

WHO WAS DUSTY?

With the British group The Springfields, Dusty Springfield entered the heart of swinging London in the 1960s. "You Don't Have to Say You Love Me" (1966) and "Son of a Preacher Man" are two of her solo hits (1969). She saw her career revived after a period of drug and alcohol abuse thanks to the 1987 Pet Shop Boys song "What Have I Done to Deserve This?" and the Scandal soundtrack.

Dusty Springfield was a British singer who, like the Motown sounds she adored, modeled her look and voice after. She was born Mary Isabel Catherine Bernadette O'Brien on April 16, 1939, in London, England.

She always had a passion for music. She and her older brother Dion started singing together when she was a little child in the garage of their parents. They enjoyed making music together, and by the late 1950s, they had begun giving live performances for audiences.

After briefly performing with a cabaret act by the name of the Lana Sisters in the early 1960s, Mary reconnected with her brother to form a new group, The Springfields. Tim Field, a different vocalist with whom Dion had begun to collaborate, served as the inspiration for the moniker The Springfields that the group used. The brothers and sisters also gave themselves stage names. Her brother became Tom Springfield, and Mary became known as Dusty Springfield.

The band's folk-influenced music, which had a pop feel that would later fuel Beatlemania, came at the perfect time. The Springfields released a number of Top Five British singles, including "Say I Won't Be There" and "Island of Dreams" in 1962. (1963). With the 1962 release of "Silver Threads and Golden Needles," which peaked at No. 20 on the American charts, they even received some attention from the United States, which was unusual for British acts at the time.

CATHOLIC GIRL

In 1968, Dusty declared, "HELL, have I been a hellraiser, but now I'm settling." Those statements seemed like wishful thinking coming from a lady who had navigated the highs and lows of stardom with a wandering, talented, and restless spirit. A self-described "malcontent," her pursuit of perfection has repeatedly damaged her desire for mental tranquility and brought her into the center of both personal and political turmoil. She was born in the midst of Britain's war preparations, a cheerful schoolgirl and a sophisti- cated star. In the future, this was used as a metaphor for her difficult life.

In response to Hitler's expansionist policies, nations were rearming when Dusty was born on April 16, 1939. In the US, President Roosevelt called for peace but also supporting military defense against aggression as Russia held negotiations with Western nations in Moscow. The Territorial Army was mobilized in the parks of London, blackout curtains were hung at windows, and basements were transformed into air-raid shelters. Girls of eighteen were needed for a new 100,000-strong army of nurses. The Civil Defense Bill was hurried through Parliament despite claims of "peace in our time."

Mary Isobel Catherine O'Brien was born in a big, drafty Victorian home in north London amid all this elation and frantic speculation. The family residence shown on her birth certificate is 87 Fordwych Road in West Hampstead, which in the 1930s was a symbol of middle-class mobility. The detached homes of West Hampstead and Cricklewood represented a "step up" from working-class Kilburn with its sizable Irish immigrant community.

Catherine Anne Ryle, better known as Kay to her friends, was Dusty's strong-willed mother and an Irishwoman. She was a flapper girl in the 1920s and had sparkling eyes and a pointed pixie face. She was also of noble descent. Her grandparents reportedly were part of a traveling Gilbert and Sullivan troupe, and her father worked as a parliamentary correspondent for the Irish Times. Kay herself had aspirations to be a world-class entertainer, but she was only ever able to perform as a dancer in amateur dramatic productions. In the 1920s, the theatre was seen to be an unacceptable career for a respectable Catholic girl since an actress was regarded as only one step above a prostitute. The ultimate aims of the Catholic girl were marriage and motherhood, but Kay postponed both as long as she could.

At age 31, Kay fell in love with and wed Dusty's father. Gerard Anthony O'Brien, a shy, lumbering Scotsman with a moon face who went by the initials OB, was five years Kay's junior. He made a nice living as an income-tax accountant at Lauderdale Mansions in Paddington when Dusty was born. Later, he worked as a tax advisor for wealthy clientele. His genuine dream of becoming a classical concert pianist, however, continued to be blocked by this regular office labor. OB, who was raised in India and is firmly middle class, was allegedly "shoved off to public school at the age of seven." He was then sent back and forth between Britain and India until he graduated from high school. His turbulent upbringing left him reserved. Prior to beginning a family, the O'Briens waited four years. Dion—later known as Tom—was Kay's firstborn, and Mary—currently Dusty—arrived four years after Dion.

Despite having a mutual love of music, Kay and OB were not a good match due to their different temperaments. With her sharp wit and big goals, Kay couldn't stay still. In order to make up on sleep throughout the day, she would stay late hours and have tea parties at five in the morning. The personal secretary of Dusty and one of her closest friends, Pat Rhodes, asserts that Dusty did that as well. When we went to bed at twelve o'clock, she would be lazing around and watching television. No matter what time she was supposed to go to bed, she genuinely couldn't sleep at conventional hours.

According to Pat, OB's slow-burning sensitivity irked Kay and caused nasty arguments. Even though they didn't get along and were often bickering, despite their extreme discontent, they were Catholics and would never have considered divorce. I had a gut feeling that Dusty used to listen to this and it was what ultimately turned her off to marriage. Dusty was a girl who threw fits and was envious of her brother. She had no memories of warmth or love. I must admit that I took the comments given extremely seriously. My brother and I have a complicated connection. Ambivalence permeated our home. fierce ambivalence!

She was "very angry" and called her father a "lazy sod." She would be crushed by his insults. I can still picture myself entering the front room and clinging to the hot water pipes until they scalded me and my palms turned bright red. And nobody ever paid attention," stated Dusty. I'm not sure what motivated my behavior.I may have sensed the tension and believed I was to blame. Just prior to the singer's passing, Angela Hunter, Dusty's first cousin, disagreed, telling me that OB was a "kind, nice, extremely humorous man." I recall him picking Dusty up every night from a Chelsea nightclub where she was performing in order to take her back on the final Tube.

Dusty was restless all the time: when her family moved to the home counties, her parents never unpacked because they missed London so much. 'My father never cut the grass; the chickens of the neighbors used to go in there.' They kept saying, "We're going back to London." They were trapped in being suburban without having suburban minds.'

Dusty inherited her mother's vivacious, impulsive personality, as well as her father's tense shyness and angry self-discipline. Her two personalities declared war on each other at a young age. Her mother was full of Irish proverbs and stern moral admonitions, such as 'Ingratitude will show on your face' and 'The best things you can do are for other people.' She was also known for hurling objects around the room and once slapped a trifle with a spoon very hard, saying, 'You'll get it faster this way.' Dusty struggled constantly between the desire to please and the desire to be completely selfish, caught between highly talented parents and her Catholic upbringing.

Tom, her brother, was an introverted musician. He inherited his father's sensitivity and, as a means of defense, acquired a polite reserve, expressing his emotions through music. He and Dusty started experimenting with sounds at a young age. Tim Feild, a former member of Springfield, subsequently observed, "They had thought of nothing but show business since they were four years old." Tom and Dusty would compose music on the kitchen table using "found" instruments, such as spoons and saucepans.

They had contrasting musical ideas from the start, and it was this conflict that later served as the Springfields' creative impetus. They enjoyed a healthy childhood. Dusty was a bouncing infant who was constantly tumbling out of things, emulating her energetic mother. She once dove from the pram and landed on the ground before falling off the table and landing on the kitchen floor. She radiated a vibrant knowledge of her surroundings. She once remarked, "I remember the low drones of planes after a bombing assault." "I recall attending the victory celebrations at the conclusion of the war while decked up in a white baby siren outfit. Happy smiles could be seen once more on a big table in the middle of the street filled with birthday cakes. Additionally, I recall the end of rationing and seeing my first banana when fruit supply resumed.

Up to the age of seven, Dusty was a "beautiful girl in pretty frocks," playing on the park swings and taking wild family vacations to Bognor. After contracting the measles, "everything appeared to alter." I became disgustingly overweight. She felt self-conscious and uncomfortable as she put on weight, and to add insult to injury, her short sight required her to wear the despised round pebble glasses.

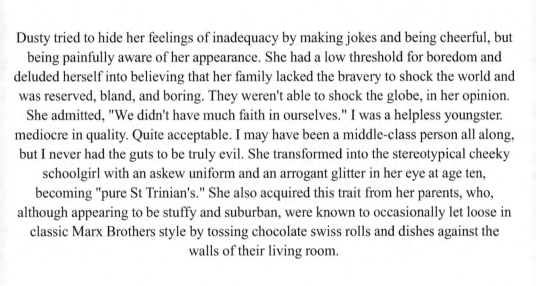

Dusty tried to hide her feelings of inadequacy by making jokes and being cheerful, but being painfully aware of her appearance. She had a low threshold for boredom and deluded herself into believing that her family lacked the bravery to shock the world and was reserved, bland, and boring. They weren't able to shock the globe, in her opinion. She admitted, "We didn't have much faith in ourselves." I was a helpless youngster. mediocre in quality. Quite acceptable. I may have been a middle-class person all along, but I never had the guts to be truly evil. She transformed into the stereotypical cheeky schoolgirl with an askew uniform and an arrogant glitter in her eye at age ten, becoming "pure St Trinian's." She also acquired this trait from her parents, who, although appearing to be stuffy and suburban, were known to occasionally let loose in classic Marx Brothers style by tossing chocolate swiss rolls and dishes against the walls of their living room.

In High Wycombe, a modest manufacturing community in Buckinghamshire, Dusty began attending school after her family relocated there. After the war, a large number of black immigrants from Trinidad and Jamaica relocated there, and it was at this time that Dusty first encountered the black American music and West Indian culture that would later capture her attention.

In the heart of the town, St. Augustine's Catholic Primary was a little institution in 1949. The teaching administrator at the time, Sister Agnes Dempsey DJ, afterwards known as Mother Marie Louise, recalled her former student Dusty with affection forty years later: "I can still see her as a vivacious little nine-year-old, in her blue blazer." She had rust-gold colored hair with a quiff that was soft and silky rather than curly. She had sparkling eyes and glasses with a gold rim. Sister Agnes, who was well into her eighties, yet had a strong memory of Dusty: "Study for her was no real hardship; her application and attention were consistent."She occasionally stayed after school to scrub the chalkboard and speak. I used to think that she would make a fantastic missionary because of her upbeat, sociable, and giving nature. Naturally, I didn't tell her about this.

Although Dusty once thought about becoming a nun (what nice Catholic girl doesn't?), she gave up the notion since she felt she could never be "good" enough. She passed the St. Bernard's Convent entrance exam at age eleven. Sister Agnes was sad to see her leave and had a motherly care for her: "At eleven she had already become a beautiful lady, with a new haircut. I was happy for her later on when I learned of her success in the entertainment industry. There is always need for modest joy spikes in this old planet.

It wasn't with much fondness that Dusty recalled her school days: "I didn't think they were the happiest days of my life and I still don't." Many challenging periods also existed.

Just a short while before the family returned to London, she attended St. Bernard's Convent. St. Bernard's was a small, private school with rather unique teaching strategies that was run by a group known as the Daughters of Jesus. As a student in the 1960s, Roisin Brozozowski recalls a run-down structure with about 200 fee-paying girls next to a sizable park near the Rye river. It ultimately had to shut down because it failed a building inspection, she said. I recall a history book from Florence Nightingale's time on the market. The quality of schooling fell short of expectations. There was a great deal of religious instruction and discussion of hell.

The Daughters of Jesus emphasized the value of doing good deeds and pushed their followers to help the ill and impoverished. The order took care of "decrepit" old people in "war huts," which were tithe cottages on the border of the school grounds, according to Roisin. They made an effort to instill a sense of giving in you. They must have produced a large number of social workers. It was rumored that the strict headmistress, Sister Fidelias, smoked a pipe, and one of the sisters had a wooden limb. But despite the strange environment, there were stringent guidelines: There was a point system, and you might lose points for things like not wearing a hat in public or speaking when you weren't supposed to. If you suffered a severe point loss, you were had to stand up in assembly while they read out your transgressions. It was very frightening. The majority of the students were of Polish, Irish, or Italian ancestry, but Roisin acknowledges that the experience was equally "character-building" for them.

Dusty was transferred from St. Bernard's to St. Anne's, a bustling, fee-paying convent in West London with more than 500 students. St Anne's closed its doors in 1987, joining the ranks of many convent schools in Britain during the 1980s and 1990s. As fewer and fewer nuns took vows and joined teaching orders, there had been a 'vocation dilemma' that had developed over time. However, the convent was thriving when Dusty enrolled in the school in 1951. It was run by the Sisters of Charity of St. Jeanne Antide Thouret, a modest but successful order.

The school served as the hub of the neighborhood, and its magazine, which featured images of resourceful females wearing gymslips, served as a focal point. On the day of Queen Elizabeth's coronation in 1953, a "Spiritual Bouquet" was delivered to her "as a testimony of our respect... God's blessing on her reign." That year, during the school's

Golden Jubilee celebrations, editor Angela Talbot White pondered: "We wonder whether the school will develop as much as it has over the past fifty years the great and indefatigable spirit of the Sisters, who continually set us the excellent example of practicing the school motto, virtus sola nobilitas est [Goodness Is Excellence]."

The school magazine had a fresh note in it within two years. It was urged that we "live up to our reputation." Members typically exhibit a lack of selflessness and a too casual attitude toward their Houses, so a stronger feeling of allegiance to each House is required. But by this time, the first waves of the beat generation and rock 'n' roll had already begun to drift over the Atlantic, giving the post-war teenage population a new feeling of identity. Dusty struggled between being a model student and having fun because convent education promoted both good deeds and sexual sublimation in equal measure. Dusty felt compelled to uphold the school motto. Dusty struggled throughout her life like many ex-convent girls do, swinging between nun-like eccentricity and wild rebellion. According to Margaret Regan, who attended the same London Catholic school as Dusty, "the assumption was that even if you had a profession you would get married within a few years and definitely have children," she explains. The official position was that having children was the primary goal of marriage and that enjoying oneself came in second. Except for the rhythm method, there was no birth control, according to the Church. Additionally, there was very little sex before marriage, and women were expected to dress modestly. Nothing you did inspired or enraged your young man. But 'having a profession was made rather appealing. You got the impression that marriage was considered second best, says Regan, even though very few girls actually had a vocation. The Virgin Mary was held up as an ex

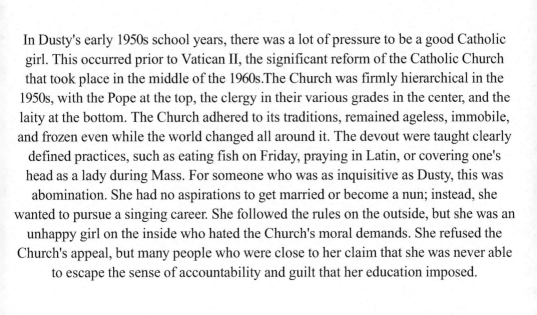

In Dusty's early 1950s school years, there was a lot of pressure to be a good Catholic girl. This occurred prior to Vatican II, the significant reform of the Catholic Church that took place in the middle of the 1960s.The Church was firmly hierarchical in the 1950s, with the Pope at the top, the clergy in their various grades in the center, and the laity at the bottom. The Church adhered to its traditions, remained ageless, immobile, and frozen even while the world changed all around it. The devout were taught clearly defined practices, such as eating fish on Friday, praying in Latin, or covering one's head as a lady during Mass. For someone who was as inquisitive as Dusty, this was abomination. She had no aspirations to get married or become a nun; instead, she wanted to pursue a singing career. She followed the rules on the outside, but she was an unhappy girl on the inside who hated the Church's moral demands. She refused the Church's appeal, but many people who were close to her claim that she was never able to escape the sense of accountability and guilt that her education imposed.

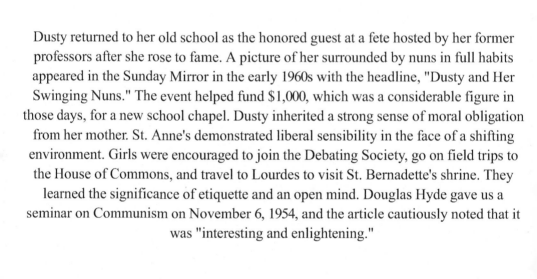

Dusty returned to her old school as the honored guest at a fete hosted by her former professors after she rose to fame. A picture of her surrounded by nuns in full habits appeared in the Sunday Mirror in the early 1960s with the headline, "Dusty and Her Swinging Nuns." The event helped fund $1,000, which was a considerable figure in those days, for a new school chapel. Dusty inherited a strong sense of moral obligation from her mother. St. Anne's demonstrated liberal sensibility in the face of a shifting environment. Girls were encouraged to join the Debating Society, go on field trips to the House of Commons, and travel to Lourdes to visit St. Bernadette's shrine. They learned the significance of etiquette and an open mind. Douglas Hyde gave us a seminar on Communism on November 6, 1954, and the article cautiously noted that it was "interesting and enlightening."

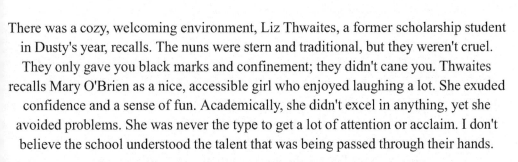

There was a cozy, welcoming environment, Liz Thwaites, a former scholarship student in Dusty's year, recalls. The nuns were stern and traditional, but they weren't cruel. They only gave you black marks and confinement; they didn't cane you. Thwaites recalls Mary O'Brien as a nice, accessible girl who enjoyed laughing a lot. She exuded confidence and a sense of fun. Academically, she didn't excel in anything, yet she avoided problems. She was never the type to get a lot of attention or acclaim. I don't believe the school understood the talent that was being passed through their hands.

Dusty was struggling at the moment to shed the puppy fat. She had plump tiny legs that were incredibly straight, and according to Thwaites, her favorite shoes were those hideous sandals with the bar and punches on the front. You would never in a million years have predicted that she would become well-known. She had zero concern for how she looked. Later in life, Dusty struggled with weight issues and was plagued by the memory of the overweight schoolgirl. Anxious by nature, she relied heavily on chocolate to calm herself.

Dusty and Liz Thwaites attended the same school, St Jeanne- Antide's, which was proud of its cooperative spirit but frequently expressed shock at the quantity of black marks the sisters received. "At studies, we are advancing steadily... Let's hope this continues and the number of black marks the House receives decreases at the same time,' Cecilia Trasler, the house captain, said hastily in 1954.

Dusty and Liz Thwaites attended the same school, St Jeanne- Antide's, which was proud of its cooperative spirit but frequently expressed shock at the quantity of black marks the sisters received. "At studies, we are advancing steadily... Let's hope this continues and the number of black marks the House receives decreases at the same time,' Cecilia Trasler, the house captain, said hastily in 1954.

Dusty wasn't athletic, despite the fact that St. Jeanne-frequently Antide's competed academically and athletically with the other houses, St. Anne's and St. Michael's. She only really put any effort into it during her fourth year when she joined the school hockey team. She is smiling and holding her hockey stick between her legs in the team shot, sitting up straight, with short hair and glasses. But the year wasn't great: "We played very few hockey matches last Easter term owing to lack of practice, and regrettably those we did play were not particularly successful," said the games captain in the school magazine. We lost all but three of the first XI at the start of the new academic year, thus the majority of the new team had only played hockey for a year. This might have been the cause of our only match's demise.

Dusty was not a sports enthusiast and left athletics to the more athletic females, despite her valiant efforts on the hockey ice. She took lessons but, although being a die-hard tennis fan in the 1970s, avoided playing whenever she could. Her friend Pat Rhodes claims, "She was a lazy person. She would work extremely hard and sweat for an hour on stage, but she would not run around a field. Furthermore, Dusty had little desire to excel in the classroom. Though she had never enjoyed lessons, she lacked the guts to lie. Not that it's a brave thing to do, she added. I like learning French, English, and history. I had trouble getting through O Level, I disliked the book they assigned me to read, Mansfield Park, so I developed a dislike for English as a result. The American Hollywood author Budd Schulberg had my undivided attention.

Different thoughts about Dusty's academic value were held by her math teacher, Mrs. Denise Garvey. According to Mrs. Garvey, she was "really an all-rounder," very intelligent, and good in math. She loved to play practical pranks and was a social butterfly who loved sports. Mary could always be seen having fun somewhere. Even though Dusty didn't particularly like school, she was good at winning over the teachers while still maintaining her friends' favor. Her true passion was music, though: "Whenever she had the opportunity, she would be playing the guitar and learning country and western songs," Mrs.Gravy.

THE SPRINGFIELD STORY

DUSTY'S YEARS OF POP apprenticeship started virtually as soon as she graduated from high school. She did, however, at first briefly consider acting. She frequently attended plays at the Old Vic theater in London and aspired to be a Shakespearean actress. She decided to join in classes at Jane Campbell's acting school in Ealing with this in mind. She was only around for two weeks. I was miming, making an attempt at acting for the first time. I discovered that I was not a good mime and that I could not open a window if the window was not present.

She thought about singing again and made the decision to work in many musical genres to obtain as much real-world experience as she could. Having been born with this peculiar tiny voice, "I knew my chances were higher." She sang duets with Tom using the "weird tiny voice," and they collaborated on songs and vocal arrangements during their free time as she continued to work her "day jobs." Dusty worked in a laundry, a record store, and at Bentall's department store, where she sold buttons, dustbins, and electric train sets, while biding her time until the big break arrived. When she accidentally blew the fuses in the lighting system of the store during a presentation, her career in retail came to an abrupt end.

Riss Chantelle's all-girl vocal group, the Lana Sisters, was in need of a new member, which was fortunate for Dusty. Chantelle had earned excellent experience playing guitar with the Ivy Benson Band, a major entry point for female musicians in Britain into jazz and studio work at the time and the top female swing band. Benson, a direct Yorkshirewoman, set strong standards for her players and always ensured that they met the highest professional standards. The Tracy Sisters, Sheila Tracy's brass duo, and Gracie Cole's All Girl Orchestra are a few of the most outstanding individuals who later went on to start their own bands. After spending a lot of time touring with Benson in Europe and Egypt, Chantelle joined forces with a friend, Lynne Abrams, to start her own act. She then placed an ad in the Stage for a third Lana Sister.

A letter from Mary O'Brien, who had a nice sounding name, was one of the responses she got. Dusty seemed to write in a way that fit. According to the late Chantelle"she came over as a well-educated girl, someone you could have a good conversation with."

I immediately said yes when she came in for an audition at one of our practice spaces in Leicester Square. I wanted her to be the bottom voice in the trio because of how deep her voice was. Between Lynne and I, I was the middle harmony. The sound was flawless as we sang together. Our empathy for one another grew quickly. Dusty moved in with Lynne's parents in Hertford because her parents were living in Brighton at the time and she needed to be nearer to London. They were quickly scheduled for a Southern Music Publishing audition by Chantelle. We performed some of our songs one evening at six o'clock. We immediately began to be videotaped.

They signed with Fontana, then a division of the major label Philips, in 1959. Philips later acquired the Springfields and Dusty as a solo artist. The Lana Sisters' smooth jazzy pop fit in well with variety tours and TV appearances, and promotion got underway. Their co-manager, Adam Faith's manager and renowned showbiz matriarch Evelyn Taylor, promoted their light-hearted vaudeville approach. Dusty later recalled: "She was in a seedy little office taking bookings for American airbases. It was operated by Joe Collins, the father of Jackie and Joan."

One of their first bookings was for the early BBC pop program Six-Five Special, which combined sport, comedy, and music for jiving teenagers and served as a forerunner to the illustrious Ready, Steady, Go! From Joe Brown and the Bruvvers to Don Lang and His Frantic Five, all the popular bands of the time participated. This early TV exposure offered Dusty a taste of the developing glamorous pop scene, which fueled her determination to succeed. Dusty remarked, "We didn't have hits, but we had records." It gave me knowledge of microphone and television techniques, as well as lighting setups.

Alongside Adam Faith, the girls also made an appearance on BBC's Drumbeat. They participated in a Tommy Steele Christmas Spectacular on television, singing "Seven Little Girls Sitting on the Back Seat" with Al Saxon, appeared at benefit performances, and supported Nat King Cole during his London performances. (Chantelle remembers, "He was smashing, a really nice man.")

Dusty barely spent a year touring with the Lana Sisters, but in that time, she gained a wide variety of expertise by taking any available gigs. "We scheduled it, performed in it, drove it, "Declaring with pride. The heart of music publishing, Denmark Street, was bursting with energy in 1959. Before you even got out of the car, publishers would run up to you and say, "Here's a song for your next broadcast!" we would get in the car and head down there. We would carry acetates on our way home from town."

The Lana Sisters released upbeat, lighthearted songs like "Chimes of Arcady," "Buzzin'," and "and "Tell Him No," as well as evocative crooners like "My Mother's Eyes." "We did that for every mother," "Chantelle stated. "It was hilarious." We had to sing frantically and quickly, but we could also drag the notes out into jazzy phrasing. We had complete freedom and diligently worked on our harmonies.

Dusty learned a lot about stagecraft from Chantelle. Although dressed in silver lurex, Dusty was meant to have an air of refinement. She was barred from falling down steps, dropping glasses and saucers, or whistling in the dressing room. Dusty added, "Riss was quite patient with me." She struggled to fit in sometimes and laughed sarcastically about it now. We used to wear pale-blue tulle skirts with silver lame drawstrings, which we would yank halfway through the performance to throw back our skirts like flashers and reveal the little lame numbers underneath.

Chantelle maintained her composure despite reports that Dusty's split from the Lana Sisters was contentious. She needed the experience of being in a group to get her where she was, and I believe she wanted to be a solo artist. She was familiar with the recording studios, the road trips, and the highs and lows. Many people believe it will be simple, but she saw it as a job, much like an accountant or a lawyer. "I hated it when they hinted that I was letting them down, but I had to go on," Dusty remarked in regards to leaving the organization. In order to succeed, especially in show business, you occasionally have to let people down. And after the Springfields arrived, the only person who had previously entered a stage was myself. Thus, it was a good, challenging training.

She accepted an invitation to join their new act as a permanent member from Tim Feild and Dusty's brothers Tom and Dusty at the beginning of 1960. At London's high class club run by Helene Cordet, Tom met Tim while playing a date. Tim, a vocalist, agreed to fill in when a temporary partner became ill. Following the performance, the two realized they had similar passions for folk, Latin, and African music. They made the choice to collaborate.

Tom was then prepared to give up his day job and focus only on music. I never had piano lessons, but I began playing by ear at a very young age and had what seemed to be a sense of harmony,' he said. "I became a professional after being fired from every job I applied for. Office work was beyond hope for me! Before joining the band, Tim Feild had likewise marched through a number of careers. He was an Old Etonian and began his career in the Navy. He tried wine tasting, advertising, stockbroking, and public relations after being demobilized, but none of these were really exciting to him. In 1957, he embarked on a globe tour with his guitar in tow. He busked to make money while traveling more than 20,000 miles through the USA, Japan, and the Far East. He even gave waterski lessons to Elizabeth Taylor's kids in Spain. But his proudest moment was being the only representative of England at the International Folk Festival in Lahore, West Pakistan.

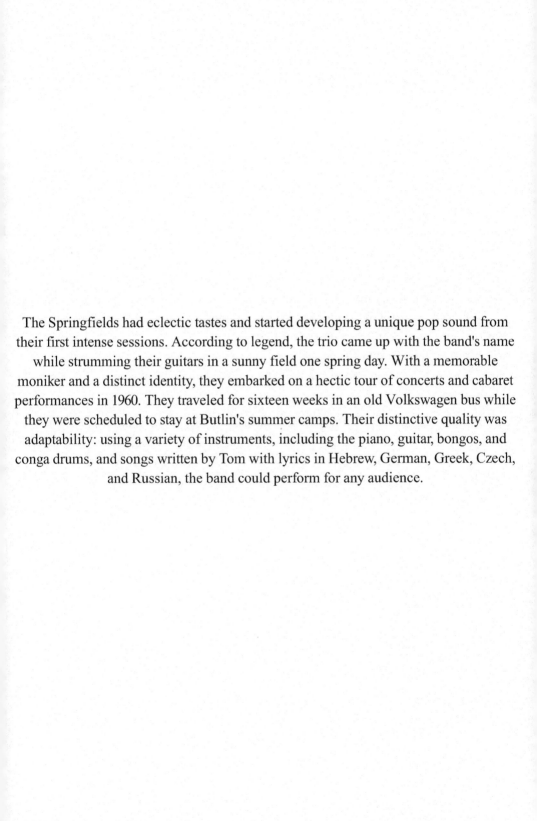

The Springfields had eclectic tastes and started developing a unique pop sound from their first intense sessions. According to legend, the trio came up with the band's name while strumming their guitars in a sunny field one spring day. With a memorable moniker and a distinct identity, they embarked on a hectic tour of concerts and cabaret performances in 1960. They traveled for sixteen weeks in an old Volkswagen bus while they were scheduled to stay at Butlin's summer camps. Their distinctive quality was adaptability: using a variety of instruments, including the piano, guitar, bongos, and conga drums, and songs written by Tom with lyrics in Hebrew, German, Greek, Czech, and Russian, the band could perform for any audience.

By 1961, the initial wave of rock 'n' roll hysteria had passed, only to be replaced by a desire for softer, more melodic pop music. Johnny Franz, a down-to-earth cockney who worked for Philips, invited the group to audition. The Springfields hesitantly played guitars and performed their rendition of "Dear John," an 1860s American Civil War hymn, at their first informal session. Franz was so impressed that he immediately signed them, took them into the studio, and released their debut single, "Dear John."

Johnny Franz played a vital part in both Dusty's later solo career and the success of the Springfields. He was one of pop's hidden heroes, a smart, kind man. In 1977, while he was in his fifties and suffering from a heart attack, a particular recording tradition came to an end. "I had the utmost respect for him." According to Dave Shrimpton, production manager of Philips in the 1960s, he was a member of the "old guard" of house producers. "He knew what he had to do, therefore he got on with it fairly successfully."

Although "Dear John" wasn't a big hit, it made the Springfields more well-known. They were listed as one of the "Ten Future Star Attractions" in an NME article that year. Only the Springfields out of the ten named, which also featured Danny Williams, Anita Scott, Russ Sainty, and the Krew Kats, found permanent success. They stood out amid the balladeers, crooners, and subpar rock 'n' rollers with their crisp instrumentation and unique harmonies. After touring the nation and presenting numerous small-scale shows, they started their first lengthy, six-week tour with musician and comedian Charlie Drake. Their second single, "Breakaway," peaked at no. 31 in the British charts in July and remained there for eight weeks, greatly raising their prominence on the cabaret and variety circuit.

The Springfields' oddball appeal landed them radio spots on Parade of the Pops, Saturday Club, and Easy Beat, while TV appearances on Thank Your Lucky Stars and The Benny Hill Show brought them to a wide-ranging family audience. Dusty told the Observer, "We received TV exposure really rapidly." "We found that if you sang loud and quickly, everyone was incredibly impressed." We were incredibly happy. It was crucial to have a positive attitude. They were careful not to let their cynicism show if it was there behind the smiles.

By the time the Springfields' third hit, "Bambino," was released, they had amassed a sizable cross-section of admirers. "Bambino," a suitably schmaltzy remake of a centuries-old Neapolitan Christmas carol, was released in time for Christmas in 1961. To make it a huge bestseller, Tom had updated and retitled it. It spent three months on the charts and peaked at No. 16 in the UK Top 20.

With thus much exposure, the Springfields appeared out of nowhere to win Best Vocal Group in NME's end-of-year Popularity Poll and Top Vocal-Instrumental Group in Melody Maker. They defeated favorites like the Mudlarks and the Dallas Boys as well as previous champions, the King Brothers. Tom exclaimed breathlessly, "We're amazed!" afterward. Our feet haven't touched the earth since we got the news.

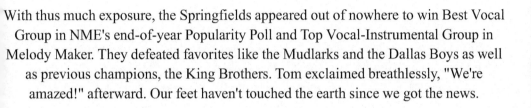

The Springfields were praised as being representative of pop culture's new middle class. The fact that Dusty was a former convent girl and that the lads had worked at Lloyds attracted a lot of attention. According to 1960s hipster magazine Scene, "They've replaced that armpit-scratching school whose interviews had to be extensively controlled by their trainers." Due of her upbringing, Dusty felt restrained: When you're middle class, you always worry about what others will think and say if you do something unconventional, like singing about love and passion in front of a crowd of a thousand, she added. Working class people don't think that way because they want to prove something to the outside world. And no one doubts the upper classes when they do this just for laughs.

The year 1962 proved crucial for The Springfields' popularity in the US, indicating that they were prepared to make an international splash. Their following two singles, "Goodnight Irene" and "Silver Threads and Golden Needles," which combined country music and harmony, helped them break into the American market. On the latter, Dusty's voice first appears with a new, soulful edge, a sign of the course she would eventually take. In addition to reaching the top spot in New Zealand and Australia, "Silver Threads" also quickly entered the US Top 20.

Particularly pleased with their influence in America, the Springfields expressed it. You have no idea how shocked we were when "Silver Threads" cracked the US Hot 100, Tom admitted to NME. "When it failed to chart here after we recorded it for Britain, we lost heart. We're working hard right now to fast adapt! It's amazing how an American hit can start everything off. The proposals have already begun to pour in quickly." By mid-1962, however, it seemed that audiences had grown weary of the drawling nasal style popularized by the Everly Brothers, despite the fact that vocal groups were still popular in America thanks to the developing R&B movement.

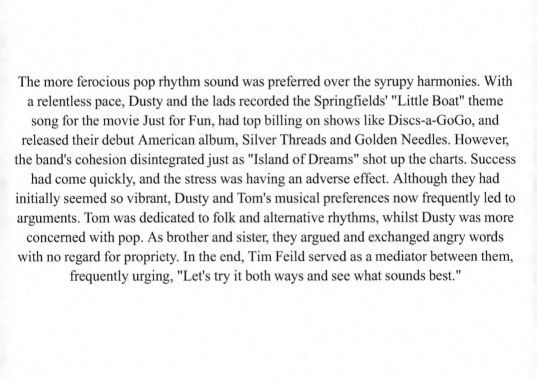

The more ferocious pop rhythm sound was preferred over the syrupy harmonies. With a relentless pace, Dusty and the lads recorded the Springfields' "Little Boat" theme song for the movie Just for Fun, had top billing on shows like Discs-a-GoGo, and released their debut American album, Silver Threads and Golden Needles. However, the band's cohesion disintegrated just as "Island of Dreams" shot up the charts. Success had come quickly, and the stress was having an adverse effect. Although they had initially seemed so vibrant, Dusty and Tom's musical preferences now frequently led to arguments. Tom was dedicated to folk and alternative rhythms, whilst Dusty was more concerned with pop. As brother and sister, they argued and exchanged angry words with no regard for propriety. In the end, Tim Feild served as a mediator between them, frequently urging, "Let's try it both ways and see what sounds best."

Feild's friendly disposition helped to diffuse the group's stress, even if he found the circumstances difficult. He once bemoaned Dusty's performance attire. They used to aggravate him beyond measure, he admitted. She like unusual designs that call for at least 14 stiff petticoats. As a real grande dame, Dusty absolutely refused to let me carry her petticoats into and out of the theaters, which made me angry. Later, Dusty claimed that he had only been joking and that the gang had been making a lot of fun of her skirts.

When Feild's wife Rachel became unwell at the end of 1962, he had to leave the group to take care of her. His replacement, Mike Longhurst-Pickworth, also known as Mike Hurst, a genial and talkative young man of twenty-one, was already close with the group. Pat Rhodes reflects, "It was a shame Tim left. Although he was fairly abrasive, Mike Hurst got along with everyone. He didn't blend in as well as Tim did because of his outspoken demeanor. Tim went, and the ambiance in the song vanished. Personally, it was no longer the Springfields. Always on guard, Dusty maintained a façade of upbeat enthusiasm. She stayed in touch with her old school, St. Anne's in Ealing, and wrote a little essay for the magazine for alumnae in the fall of 1962. She wrote, "Show business is enjoyable but requires tremendous hard effort." A typical day in town starts around 8 a.m. with a hair appointment (I'm typing this at the hairdresser's). Following this, there will likely be a press conference, a quick lunch, and an afternoon practice and recording session. Then there will be another practice for the evening show. Many people in show business are "interesting and charming," she adds respectfully. It's remarkable to see how many celebrities are Catholics, like Max Bygraves, Joan Turner,

Dickie Henderson, and Anne Shelton. ' She shares a few "on-the-road" anecdotes, including one about the time the band was on tour and stopped in a Scottish little town with two dance halls. The other hall quickly filled up once word spread that the Springfields were in the first one. The Springfields' microphone and lighting system were 'left in utter darkness and we three huddled behind the drum kit warding off enraged Scots' when the owners of the vacant venue scurried over and fused them. The boredom of lengthy journeys and demanding schedules was lessened by incidents like this, which also reduced rising friction within the band.

At the recording of "Island of Dreams," Mike Hurst performed with the Springfields for the first time on vinyl. He had been chosen from a competitive round of auditions as a trainee insurance broker who played rock and roll at gatherings. At the height of the Springfields' success, he was thrown into the deep end despite being eager, self-assured, and prepared to learn. According to Pat Rhodes, "On the surface, things appeared to be fine, but I don't think they actually got along. When he joined, there were a few more disagreements. Since he was much younger, he lacked showbiz experience.

By recording a Christmas EP on Philips for Woman's Own magazine, The Springfields increased their appeal to general audiences. They ran the risk of limiting themselves to a world of uninspired easy listening with their swinging interpretations of classic carols like "The Twelve Days of Christmas" and "Mary's Boy Child." At the conclusion of 1962, when they were granted the chance to record an album in Nashville, the birthplace of country music, everything changed. Shelby Singleton, who ran Sun Records in Nashville in the 1980s, was in charge of bringing the Springfields to the United States. In the 1950s and 1960s, Singleton, a former A&R manager with Philips' subsidiary Mercury, spent a lot of time searching Europe for artists who would be commercially successful in the United States. I brought numerous European performers to Nashville, including Nana Mouskouri and Johnny Hallyday. And many black American artists were keen to learn more about Europe. Therefore, whenever we could, we were expanding the scope of our recording. In 1988, the late Singleton told me, "We wanted to make international hits."

SOLO CAREER

The Springfields split up in the latter part of 1963, paving the way for Springfield to start a lucrative solo career. Springfield remained a constant in the pop charts for the following five years. The run of success started in January 1964 with the hit song "I Only Want to Be With You," which peaked at No. 4 in the U.K. and No. 12 in the U.S., just a few months after The Springfields split up.

Springfield produced a succession of top songs between 1965 and 1968, including "Some of Your Lovin'," "Little by Little," and the immensely popular "You Don't Have To Say You Love Me."

The album Dusty in Memphis, which she recorded with legendary music producer Jerry Wexler, who also worked on albums by Aretha Franklin and Ray Charles, marked the height of her success in 1968. The singer had long admired artists like Mavis Staples and Aretha Franklin, and she had long been a fan of both.

Black performers from the first half of the 1960s had a significant influence on her, she reportedly remarked. "The majority of the Stax performers were also favorites of mine. Mavis Staples was someone I really wanted to be. They had something in common that I hadn't heard on English radio: a certain type of strength."The performance of Dusty in Memphis was a huge hit. It rose to No. 10 on the U.S. charts thanks to "Son of a Preacher Man," one of Springfield's biggest songs. When Quentin Tarantino's movie Pulp Fiction featured that song as one of its featured tracks in 1994, it experienced a second surge in popularity.

10 ESSENTIAL FACT ABOUT DUSTY

A diva, Dusty Springfield. She was one of the greatest female vocalists to come out of Britain and Ireland, and Amy Winehouse and Adele were just a couple of the musicians that were influenced by her renowned, eerie voice. Her battle with her sexuality and misdiagnosed bipolar disorder meant she endured many difficult times, and at one point left her practically penniless. Her fierce intelligence, musical knowledge, and stance against racism and injustice frequently brought her into conflict with the chauvinistic old-fashioned music industry of the time. Here are 10 key details regarding Dusty...

DUSTY WASN'T HER REAL NAME.

Dusty Springfield, whose parents were Irish and Scots-Irish, was born Mary Catherine Isobel Bernadette O'Brien in London on April 16, 1939. Kay, Dusty's mother, was born in Dublin and raised in Tralee. Maurice Patrick Ryle, Dusty's great-grandfather, was a well-known journalist who served as editor of the Irish Independent and Evening Herald in the 1920s. He was a well-known "Redmonite" who fought for home rule, but he passed away in 1935, four years before his granddaughter was born.

AT AGE 16,SHE GAVE HERSELF A MAKEOVER

At St. Anne's convent school in Enfield, Dusty was an unattractive teen with short red hair and big glasses. She credited it with inspiring her to play the "blues" for the first time in a school assembly, but once she left at 16, she immediately discarded the Mary O'Brien image and astonished her classmates by turning up as a gorgeous, fully-made-up blonde. She claimed that Mary O'Brien "wasn't going to make it" and had been intended to become a librarian.

HER CHILDHOOD WAS EVERYTHING BUT PERFECT.

Even though she traveled to the United States with her parents on tour as a young singer and frequently visited them, Dusty subsequently claimed to have had a very sad upbringing. Her father was a severe enforcer who would hit her, and her parents were stuck in an unhappy marriage. But they also gave her a great love of music: Dusty's father, Gerard O'Brien, was a skilled pianist who appreciated both blues and classical music, and the two of them frequently passed the afternoons at the movies viewing musicals with her mother.

SHAN WAS HER FIRST STAGE NAME.

When Dusty joined the all-girl singing group the Lana Sisters in 1958, her original stage name was "Shan." Although Dusty had previously performed in small bars in London with her brother Dion, her major break came when she joined the Lana Sisters. They recorded the songs Seven Little Girls and Tell Him No (Sitting in the Back Seat). Dusty remembered, "We didn't have hits, but we did have recordings. Instructed by the group's seasoned leader Riss Chantelle, Dusty got a record deal, made an appearance on the BBC, went on tour, and sang as a backup singer for Nat King Cole.

SHE WANTED TO MAKE PEOPLE DANCE

I Only Want To Be With You, a song written by Ivor Raymonde and Mike Hawker for Hawker's then-wife, Jean Ryder, was Dusty's debut solo album, published in November 1963. Dusty wanted her first single to be a song that people could dance to and she had already rejected Money (That's What I Want) and Wishin and Hopin'. She was inspired by the success of The Twist and Dancing in the Street. The backing singer for many of Dusty's early recordings and concerts, Jean Ryder, recalled her quiet, insecure personality as well as a musical perfectionism that frequently put her at odds with male session musicians and the sexist record business.

SHE HAD PROBLEMS WITH HER SEXUALITY.

During a magazine interview in 1970, Dusty came out as bisexual, or, as she put it, "as likely to be seduced by a girl as a boy." She struggled to accept her sexuality and frequently regretted giving an interview that resulted in comments and rumors for the rest of her life, despite the fact that she was lesbian and had never had any meaningful romantic connections with men. In violation of their shared religious beliefs, Dusty once kissed his long-term California girlfriend on a balcony overlooking the Vatican.

SHE WAS A HUGE FAN OF BLUES

Dusty loved Black American music, and she was one of the key figures in introducing Motown to Britain. She began listening to the Blues with her father when she was a young child. At the Brooklyn Fox in New York, where she had shared the stage with several Motown performers, she and Martha Reeves became good friends. After refusing to perform for segregated audiences as the first white musician, Dusty later headlined the Motown Revue on British television and was expelled from Apartheid South Africa.

Her strongest album was a difficult one.

The 1968 release, Dusty in Memphis, was one of Dusty's most iconic albums and may have been her greatest musical achievement. Although it was a problematic album, Dusty was notorious for her wild partying and claimed she was too afraid to sing in the Memphis studio where Aretha Franklin had recorded some of her biggest singles. Although Dusty produced the iconic tune Son of a Preacher Man, the album did not find commercial success and she later recorded her vocals in New York.

She was insecure about how she looked.

After her early appearances as a compere on Ready, Steady, Go!, where she interviewed The Beatles among others and quickly became a Sixties icon with her instantly recognizable blonde beehive, black eye make-up, cool glamour, and signature hand gestures, Dusty was taken in by the Mods. Dusty was naturally reserved and rarely went to the fad parties and clubs of the 1960s, despite her fame. She continued to feel extremely self-conscious about the way she looked, loathing her chin and knees, and frequently expressing how Burt Lancaster-like she believed she appeared.

She wanted to scatter her ashes in Ireland.

Soon after finishing the production of her final album, A Very Fine Love in Nashville in 1994, Dusty learned she had breast cancer. She had treatment, but the cancer came back, and she passed away in Henley in March 1999. A portion of Dusty's ashes will be strewn out to sea from her favorite location, the Cliffs of Moher, by her brother Tom, according to a statement she made in her final interview with the New York Times.

TROUBLED YEAR's

Following Dusty's departure for Memphis, Springfield's career was erratic. She moved to America in 1970 after having a lifelong fascination with the country and being a bit of a Civil War nerd. But in her new home, life just became more difficult. Due to her drug troubles and other personal issues, Springfield was unable to regain her prior level of prominence.

She did carry on recording, and there were a few lone instances of success. When she collaborated with the Pet Shop Boys on the tune "What Have I Done to Deserve This" in 1987, she introduced herself to a whole new generation of music lovers. She again received modest radio playing two years later with the song "Nothing Has Been Prove" for the film Scandal.

FINAL YEAR'S AND DEATH

Springfield's final studio album, A Very Fine Love, was released in 1995 after she moved back to England in the early 1990s. She received a cancer diagnosis in the same year. Her subsequent health issues became a recurring theme in her life.

But in her later years, she developed a fresh enthusiasm for her work and career. The Dusty Springfield Anthology Collection, a 3-CD collection, was released in 1997 by Mercury Records. Rhino Records issued a limited edition of Dusty in Memphis two years later.

Springfield received its induction into the Rock & Roll Hall of Fame in 1999. On March 2 of the following year, 1999, she succumbed to cancer.

Printed in Great Britain
by Amazon

24160963R00030